Y0-BWY-079

·EVE·

*God's Word
for Women
Today*

Presented to

_____

_____

_____

*Now the man called his wife's
name Eve (Lifespring), because she was
the mother of all human beings.*

Gen. 3:20

A
MERIDIAN
Publication

WORLD
Bible Publishers

Compiled by Gwen Weising

Book and cover design by Gayle Raymer

Copyright © 1990 by Meridian.
All rights reserved.

EV1	Slimline Pocket Paperback	0-529-06859-1
EV2WB	Wedgewood Blue Bonded Leather	0-529-06860-5
EV2TT	Tropical Teal Bonded Leather	0-529-06861-3
EV2GP	Georgia Peach Country Cloth	0-529-06862-1
EV2DR	Dusty Rose Bonded Leather	0-529-06864-8
EV2WT	White Country Cloth	0-529-06865-6
EV2PB	Powder Blue Country Cloth	0-529-06866-4
EV3	Large Gift Edition	0-529-06972-5

Published by Meridian, Grand Rapids, MI

Published with World Bible Publishers

Manufactured in the United States of America

DEDICATED

...to my mother through whom God first taught (and still teaches) me his Word; to my daughter whose full life has demonstrated the vibrancy and reality of God's Word for women today; and to my twin daughters who went to be with my Lord just hours after their birth.

Gwen Weising

Gwen Weising is editor of *Aglow* magazine and Aglow Publications. She is also the author of numerous articles, and of five books including *Raising Kids on Purpose* (Revell) and *Guidance: Knowing the Will of God* (Aglow).

Abbreviations of the names of the books of the Bible

Old Testament

Gen.	— Genesis	Ec.	— Ecclesiastes
Ex.	— Exodus	Song	— Song of Solomon
Lev.	— Leviticus	Isa.	— Isaiah
Num.	— Numbers	Jer.	— Jeremiah
Deut.	— Deuteronomy	Lam.	— Lamentations
Josh.	— Joshua	Ezek.	— Ezekiel
Judg.	— Judges	Dan.	— Daniel
Ruth	— Ruth	Hos.	— Hosea
1 Sam.	— 1 Samuel	Joel	— Joel
2 Sam.	— 2 Samuel	Amos	— Amos
1 Kin.	— 1 Kings	Obad.	— Obadiah
2 Kin.	— 2 Kings	Jon.	— Jonah
1 Chr.	— 1 Chronicles	Mic.	— Micah
2 Chr.	— 2 Chronicles	Nah.	— Nahum
Ezr.	— Ezra	Hab.	— Habakkuk
Neh.	— Nehemiah	Zeph.	— Zephaniah
Esth.	— Esther	Hag.	— Haggai
Job	— Job	Zech.	— Zechariah
Ps.	— Psalms	Mal.	— Malachi
Pr.	— Proberbs		

New Testament

Mt.	— Matthew	1 Tim.	— 1 Timothy
Mk.	— Mark	2 Tim.	— 2 Timothy
Lu.	— Luke	Titus	— Titus
Jn.	— John	Philem.	— Philemon
Ac.	— The Acts	Heb.	— Hebrews
Rom.	— Romans	Jas.	— James
1 Cor.	— 1 Corinthians	1 Pet.	— 1 Peter
2 Cor.	— 2 Corinthians	2 Pet.	— 2 Peter
Gal.	— Galations	1 Jn.	— 1 John
Eph.	— Ephesians	2 Jn.	— 2 John
Phil.	— Philippians	3 Jn.	— 3 John
Col.	— Colossians	Jude	— Jude
1 Th.	— 1 Thessalonians	Rev.	— Revelation
2 Th.	— 2 Thessalonians		

All Scripture is quoted from the King James Version, unless otherwise noted. Contemporary words have been substituted (such as "you" for "ye" and "searches" for "searcheth", etc.) for clarity. Other translations are used by persmission.

NASB = New American Standard Bible

NIV = New International Version

RSV = Revised Standard Version

Eve: God's Word for Women Today is produced with the prayer that God's words may be a source of hope and encouragement in any of life's challenges.

TABLE OF CONTENTS

GOD'S GREATEST CREATION 9
   The Creation of Woman
   Boundless

GOD'S WORD FOR BRIDES &
   WIVES 15
   God's Word for Brides
   Prayer for a Young Bride
   God's Word for Wives
   God's Proverbs for Wives

GOD'S WORD FOR MOTHERS &
   GRANDMOTHERS 25
   God's Word for Mothers
   God's Proverbs for Mothers
   Dear Lord, I Do Not Ask
   God's Word for Grandmothers

GOD'S WORD FOR WIDOWS 35
   God's Love for Widows
   What Room is There?
   Jesus' Love for Widows

GOD'S WORD TO DAUGHTERS 43

WOMEN WHO WORSHIPED GOD
   IN SONG 47
   Miriam   Elizabeth
   Hannah   Mary
   Deborah   Anna

WOMEN WHO CAME TO JESUS 57
The Syrophenician Woman
Mary Who Poured Out Her Love
Martha and Mary
The Bent Woman
The Woman at the Well
The Chronically Ill Woman
Mary Magdalene

GOD'S HONOR ROLL OF WOMEN .. 71
Sarah   The Shunammite Woman
Shiphrah and Puah Esther
Jochebed   Dorcas
Rahab   Lydia
Ruth   Priscilla
Hannah   Eunice and Lois

GOD'S PROMISES TO WOMEN 107
To the Fearful
Of Wisdom
When You Feel Abandoned
To Help Women
When Your Children Leave Home
Of Security
To Poor Women
When Praying for Your Children

GOD'S GREATEST CREATION

◆

The Creation of Woman

Boundless

THE CREATION OF WOMAN

God said, "It is not good for a man to be alone; I will make a suitable helper for him."

Out of the ground the Lord formed every beast of the field and every bird of the sky. He brought them all to the man to see what he would name them; and whatever name the man gave to each living creature, that was its name.

The man gave names to all the cattle, to the birds of the sky, and to every beast of the field, but for Adam there was not found a suitable helper.

So the Lord caused a deep sleep to fall upon him. Then God took one of Adam's ribs, and afterward closed up his flesh.

And the Lord fashioned a woman from the rib he had taken from Adam, and brought her to him.

Gen. 2:18-22

And Adam said,
  "This is now bone of my bones,
  And flesh of my flesh;
  She shall be called
    Woman,
  Because she was taken out of
    Man."

Now the man called his wife's name Eve (Lifespring), because she was the mother of all the living.

Gen. 3:20

BOUNDLESS

They talk about a woman's sphere
As though it had a limit;
There's not a place in earth or
   Heaven,
There's not a task to mankind given,
There's not a blessing or a woe,
There's not a whispered yes or no,
There's not a life, or death, or
   birth,
That has a feather's weight of
   worth—
Without a woman in it.

Author Unknown

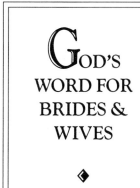

GOD'S WORD FOR BRIDES & WIVES

◆

God's Word for Brides

Prayer for a Young Bride

God's Word for Wives

God's Proverbs for Wives

There are three things
  which are too wonderful for me,
Four which I do not understand:
  The way of an eagle in the sky,
  The way of a serpent on a rock,
  The way of a ship in the middle
  of the sea,
And the way of a man with a maid.

Pr. 30:18

I will rejoice greatly
  in the Lord,
My soul will rejoice
  in my God,
For he has clothed me
  with garments of salvation,
He has wrapped me
  with a robe of righteousness,
As a bridegroom decks
  himself in wedding clothes,
And as a bride adorns herself with
  her jewels.

Isa. 61:10

If I speak with the tongues of men and of angels, but do not have love, I have become a noisy gong or a clanging cymbal.

And if I have the gift of prophecy, and know all mysteries and all knowledge; and if I have enough faith to remove mountains, but do not have love, I am nothing.

And if I give all my possessions to feed the

poor, and if I deliver my body to be burned, but do not have love, it profits me nothing.

Love is patient, love is kind, and is not jealous; love does not brag and is not arrogant, does not act unbecomingly; it does not seek its own way, is not provoked, does not take into account a wrong suffered, does not rejoice in unrighteousness, but rejoices with the truth; bears all things, believes all things, hopes all things, endures all things.

Love never fails; but if there are gifts of prophecy, they will be done away; if there are tongues, they will cease; if there is knowledge, it will be done away with.

For we know in part, and we prophesy in part; but when the perfect comes, the partial will come to an end.

When I was a child, I talked as a child, thought as a child, and reasoned as a child. But when I became an adult, I put away childish things.

For now we see in a mirror dimly, but then face to face; now I know in part, but then I shall know fully just as I also have been fully known.

But now abide faith, hope, love, these three; but the greatest of these is love.

1 Cor. 13

PRAYER FOR A YOUNG BRIDE

Dear Lord who heeds the sparrow's wing,
She is so young, let her life sing!

Like youth, so wilful in her ways,
Guard well her acts, instruct her days.

Her love is new — in trusting hands
She holds its multi-coloured strands.

Grant her a wisdom that she weaves
Her pattern well. For life deceives,

And things, not always what they seem,
Can twist and snarl a shining dream.

Help her, in testing time, to know
Love must be quick, and anger slow.

She is so young, and sweet, and gay,
Lord, go beside her all the way!

Lee Avery

For this cause a man shall leave his father
and his mother, and shall cling to his wife;
and they shall become one flesh.

Gen. 1:23, 24

How blessed is everyone
    who reveres the Lord,
Who walks in his ways.

You will eat of the
    fruit of the labor
    of your hands;
You will be happy and it will
    be well with you.

Your wife will be like a
    fruitful vine,
    inside your house,

Your children like olive
    plants
Around your table.

Ps. 128:1-3

House and wealth are an
 inheritance from fathers,
But a prudent wife is from
 the Lord.

Pr. 19:14

A gracious woman attains
 honor....

Pr. 11:16

An excellent wife is the
 crown of her husband,
But she who acts disgracefully
 is as rottenness in his bones.

Pr. 12:4

The wise woman builds her
 house,
But a foolish one tears it down
 with her own hands.

Pr. 14:1

Who can find an excellent wife?
Her worth is far above jewels.

The heart of her husband
   trusts in her,
And he will never
   lack profit.

She does him good
   and not evil
     throughout her entire life.

She looks for wool and flax,
   and works with her willing hands.

She is like merchant ships;
   that brings her food from afar.

She rises while it is still night,
   and gives food to her household,
   and a portion to her maidens.

She inspects a field
   and buys it;
   from her earnings
   she plants a vineyard.

She strengthens herself,
   and also makes her arms strong.

She senses that her gain is good;
   she works far into the night.

She stretches out her hands
   to the staff
   which holds the wool
   for spinning,
   and her hands
   grasp the spindle.

She extends her hand
   to the poor;
   and stretches out her hands
   to the needy.

She is not afraid
   of the coming of snow,
   for her entire household
   is clothed with scarlet.

She makes clothing
   for herself;
   clothing of fine linen
   which is purple in color.

Her husband is well-known
   in the gates,
   where he sits
   among the leaders of the land.

She also makes linen garments
   to sell,
   and supplies belts
   to the tradesmen.

She is clothed with strength
   and dignity.
She smiles at the future.

She speaks with wisdom,
And words of kindness
   are on her tongue.

She carefully looks
   after her household,
   and she is never lazy.

Her children rise up
   and bless her,
   her husband also praises her,
   saying,
   "Many daughters have done nobly,
   but you excel them all."

Charm is deceitful
   and beauty is passing,
   but a woman who fears
   the Lord will be praised.

Acknowledge the product
   of her hands,
   and let her works
   give her recognition
   from the leaders
   of the land.

Pr. 31:10-31

GOD'S WORD FOR MOTHERS & GRAND-MOTHERS

God's Word for Mothers

God's Proverbs for
   Mothers

Dear Lord, I Do Not Ask

God's Word for
   Grandmothers

Children are a gift
  from the Lord;
  they are his reward.
Like arrows in the hand
  of a warrior,
  so are the children
  of one's youth.
How happy is the man
  whose quiver is full of them.
He shall not be put to shame,
  when he speaks with his enemies
  in the gate.

Ps. 127:3-5

Let our sons in their youth
  be as fullgrown plants,
  and our daughters
  like sculptured corner pillars
  fashioned as for a palace.

Ps. 144:12

Can a woman forget
  her nursing child,
  and have no compassion
  on the son of her womb?

Isa.49:15

A woman will be kept safe through child-
bearing if with self-control she continues in
faith, love, and holiness with self-restraint.

1 Tim. 3:11

The rod and reproof
   give wisdom,
   but an undisciplined child,
   who gets his own way
   brings shame to his mother.

Correct your son,
   and he will give you happiness.
He will also bring delight
   to your heart.

Pr. 29:15, 17

The father of the righteous
   will greatly rejoice,
   and he who fathers a wise son
   will be glad in him.
Let your father
   and your mother
   be glad,
   and let her rejoice
   who gave birth to you.

Pr. 23:24, 25

DEAR LORD, I DO NOT ASK

Dear Lord, I do not ask
   that Thou should'st give me

Some high work of Thine,
   some noble calling,
   or some wondrous task;

Give me a little hand
   to hold in mine;

Give me a little child
   to point the way

Over the strange, sweet path
   that leads to Thee.

Give me two shining eyes
   Thy face to see.

The only crown I ask,
   dear Lord, to wear

Is this: That I may teach
   my little child.

I do not ask
   that I may ever stand

Among the wise,
   the worthy or the great;

I only ask
   that softly, hand in hand,

My child and I
   may enter at the gate.

Author unknown

The lovingkindness of the Lord
   is from everlasting to everlasting
   on those who fear him.
   His righteousness is
   to children's children,
   to those who keep his covenant,
   and who remember
   his precepts to do them.

Ps. 103:17,18

I will extol you,
   my God, O King;
   and I will bless your name
   forever and ever.
Every day I will bless you,
   and I will praise your name
   forever and ever.

Great is the Lord,
   and highly to be praised;
   and his greatness
   is unsearchable.
One generation shall praise
   your works to another,
   and shall declare
   your mighty acts.

On the glorious splendor
   of your majesty,
   and on your wonderful works,
   I will meditate.
I will tell of your greatness.

They shall eagerly utter
    the memory
    of your abundant goodness,
    and shall shout joyfully
    of your righteousness.

The Lord is gracious and merciful;
    slow to anger,
    and great in lovingkindness.
The Lord is good to all,
    and his mercies
    are over all his works.

To make known
    to the sons of men
    your mighty acts,
    and the glory of the majesty
    of your kingdom.
Your kingdom
    is an everlasting kingdom,
    and your dominion endures
    throughout all generations.

Ps. 145:1-13

May you see
  your children's children.
Peace be upon Israel!

Ps. 128:6

We have thought
  on your lovingkindness,
  O God, in the midst
  of your temple.

As is your name,
  O God, so is your praise
  to the ends of the earth.
Your right hand
  is full of righteousness.

Tell it to the next
  generation.
For such is God,
  our God forever and ever;
  he will guide us
  until death.

Ps. 48:9, 10, 13, 14

For I am mindful of the sincere faith within
you, which first dwelt in your grandmother
Lois, and your mother Eunice, and I am
sure that it is in you as well.

And for this reason I remind you to kindle
afresh the gift of God which is in you.

2 Tim. 2:5, 6

GOD'S WORD FOR WIDOWS

God's Love for Widows

What Room is There?

Jesus' Love for Widows

For the Lord your God
  is the God of gods
  and the Lord of lords.
He is the great,
  the mighty,
  and the awesome God
  who does not show partiality,
  nor take
  a bribe.

He secures justice for the orphan
  and the widow,
  and shows his love
  for the stranger
  by giving him food and clothing.

Deut. 10:17, 18

The Lord lifts up those
  who are bowed down.
The Lord loves the righteous;
  the Lord protects strangers.
He supports the fatherless
  and widows;

Praise the Lord!

Ps. 146:8, 9, 10

Let the righteous be joyful;
  let them exult before God;
Yes, let them rejoice with gladness.
Sing to God,
  sing praises to his name.

Lift up a song to him
 who rides through the deserts.
The Lord is his name.
 be jubilant before him!

He is a father to the fatherless
 and a champion to widows,
 is God in his holy habitation.

God makes a home for the
 lonely.

Ps. 68:3, 5, 6

The Lord will tear down
 the house of the proud,
 but he protects
 the boundaries of the widow.

Pr. 15:25

"Leave your orphans behind,
 I will keep them alive;
 and let your widows
 trust in me."

Jer. 49:11

Pure and undefiled religion
 in the sight of our Father
 is this:
To look after orphans and widows
 in their trouble.

Jas. 1:27

WHAT ROOM IS THERE?

What room is there for troubled fear?
   I know my Lord, and he is near;
And he will light my candle, so
   That I may see the way I go.

There need be no bewilderment
   To one who goes where he is sent:
The traceless plain, by night and day
   I set with signs lest he should stray.

My path may cross a waste of sea,
   But that need never frighten me—
Or rivers full to very brim,
   But they are open ways to him.

My path may lead through wood at night,
   Where neither moon nor any light
Of guiding star or beacon shines;
   He will not let me miss my signs.

Lord, grant to me a quiet mind,
   That, trusting thee—for thou art kind—
I may go on without a fear,
   For thou, my Lord, are always near.

Author unknown

Once Jesus went to a city called Nain, accompanied by his disciples and a large crowd.

As he approached the gate of the city, he saw a large crowd there as well. A dead man was being carried out. The deceased was the only son of his mother, and she was a widow.

When Jesus saw her, he felt compassion for her, and said to her, "Stop weeping."

Then he came up and touched the coffin. The pallbearers came to a halt. He said, "Young man, I tell you, arise!"

The dead man sat up and began to speak. And Jesus gave him back to his mother.

Lu. 7:11-15

One day Jesus sat down in the temple opposite the treasury and began watching how the people were putting money into the treasury. Many of the rich were putting in large sums.

Then a poor widow came and put in two small copper coins, which together amounted to a total of about one cent.

He called his disciples over to him and said to them, "I can assure you, this poor widow put in more than all the rich men together;

for they all gave out of their surpluses. But this woman, out of her poverty, put in all she owned, everything she had to live on."

Mk. 12:41-44

In the course of his teaching Jesus said, "Beware of the scribes who like to walk around in long robes, and like being greeted in the market places. They like the most important seats in the synagogues, and places of honor at banquets. These men prey upon the properties of widows, and for appearance's sake offer long prayers. These will receive a severe sentence."

Mk. 12:38-40

GOD'S WORD TO DAUGHTERS

The King's daughter waits
   within the palace.
Her clothing is all interwoven
   with gold.

She will be led to the King
   in her embroidered robes.
The virgins, her escorts,
   will also accompany her.

They will go out
   with gladness and rejoicing.
They will enter
   into the King's palace.

Ps. 45:13-15

Honor your father and your mother, that
your days may be prolonged in the land
which the Lord gives you.

Ex. 20:12

Jesus said to the scribes and Pharisees,
"Moses said, 'Honor your father and your
mother. Whoever curses father or mother
must die.' But you say to your parents,
'Whatever I would have given you, I have
given to God.'

"And so you annul God's word in order to
protect your traditions."

Mk. 7:10-13

Children obey your parents, for this is right. Honor your father and mother. If you do this, then all will be well with you. Yours will be a long and happy life. This is the first commandment with a promise.

Eph. 6:1-3

WOMEN WHO WORSHIPED GOD IN SONG

Miriam

Hannah

Deborah

Elizabeth

Mary

Anna

MIRIAM

Miriam the prophetess, the sister of Aaron and Moses, took the tambourine in her hand, and all the women took their tambourines and went out with dancing.

And Miriam sang to them,

"Sing to the Lord, for he is
highly exalted.
The horse and his rider he
has hurled into the sea."

Ex. 15:20, 21

HANNAH

Then Hannah prayed and said,

My heart rejoices in the Lord;
   my strength is exalted in the Lord,
   my mouth speaks boldly
   against my enemies,
   because I rejoice
   in your salvation.
There is no one as holy as the Lord,
   indeed, there is no one
   like you,
   nor is there any rock
   like our God.
Quit talking so boastfully,
   do not let arrogant talk
   come out of your mouth.
For the Lord
   is a knowing God,
   and by him actions are weighed.
The bows of the mighty
   are shattered,
   but the feeble gird on strength.
Those who were full
   are now starving,
   but those who were hungry
   cease to hunger.
Now the barren woman gives birth
   to seven children,
   but she who has many children
   is forlorn.

The Lord kills and makes alive;
　　he brings down to the grave
　　and raises up.
The Lord makes poor and rich;
　　he brings low, he also exalts.
He raises the poor
　　from the dust,
　　he lifts the needy
　　from the ash heap
　　to make them sit with nobles,
　　and inherit a seat of honor.
For the pillars of the earth
　　are the Lord's,
　　and he set the world on them.
He keeps the feet
　　of his godly ones,
　　but the wicked ones are
　　silenced in darkness;
　　for not by might
　　shall a man prevail.
Those who contend
　　with the Lord
　　will be shattered;
　　against them he will thunder
　　in the heavens.
The Lord will judge the ends
　　of the earth;
　　and he will give strength
　　to his king,
　　and great glory
　　to his anointed one.

1 Sam. 2:1-10

DEBORAH

"Praise the Lord!
  The leaders of Israel
  led in Israel,
  and the people gladly followed!
Listen, you kings and rulers!
I will sing to the Lord,
  I will sing praises
  to the Lord God of Israel.
Lord, when you went out from Seir,
  and when you marched
  from the fields of Edom
  the earth quaked,
  the heavens poured out rain.
Even Mt. Sinai shook
  at the presence of the Lord,
  the God of Israel.
In the days of Shamgar
  and Jael,
  the highways were deserted.
Travelers went by roundabout ways.
The population of Israel dwindled,
  until I, Deborah, arose—
  a mother in Israel.
Israel chose new gods;
  war was at the gates.
But among the forty thousand
  in Israel,
  there were no shields nor spears.
My heart goes out
  to the commanders of Israel,
  who offered themselves so willingly.

Bless the Lord!
All of you who ride on white donkeys,
    and sit on rich carpets,
    and those of you who are poor
    and must walk —
      sing!
Sing among those who divide their flocks
    at the watering places.
There they shall recount
    the triumphs of the Lord,
    the righteous deeds done
    for his people in Israel.

So, Lord, let all of your enemies
    perish!
But let those who love the Lord
    shine as the sun
    in its power!

Judg. 5:2-11, 31

Elizabeth

Elizabeth, filled with the Holy
Spirit, cried out:

Oh Mary, how marvelously God
   has blessed you!
   singling you out
   from all the women in the world!

And how specially blessed is the child
   who will come from your womb!
What an honor it is for me
   to have the mother of my Lord
   visit my home!
For the instant you greeted me
   my baby leaped for joy within me!

How specially blessed is the woman
   who trusts God
   to keep his promise to her!

Lu. 1:39-45

MARY

Mary responded with an outburst of thanksgiving:

All that is within me
   praises the Lord,
   and my spirit delights in God,
   my Savior;
For he has seen fit to notice me,
   his most humble servant, a nobody!
For from now on, forever
   throughout all generations,
   the world will regard me
   as the woman God favored,
   because Almighty God
   has done great things for me.
Holy is his name!
He is merciful
   to generation after generation,
   to those who reverence him.
How powerful and strong is his arm!
How he routs the proud and the haughty!
How he disposes strong rulers
   and eliminates the ordinary!
The hungry he has filled with good things,
   but the rich go away with empty hands.
And now he has come
   to help his servant Israel.
His promise of mercy
   has not been forgotten,·
The promises he made to our ancestors,
   to Abraham and all his descendants,
   forever and forever.

Lu. 1:45-55

Anna's Thanksgiving

In the temple in Jerusalem was a prophetess, Anna, the daughter of Phanuel, a descendant of Asher. She was very old, a widow of eighty-four years whose husband died only seven years after they were married.

The temple had become her home. She never left it, for she worshiped, fasted, and prayed at all hours of the day and night.

At the very moment Simeon was blessing the child Jesus, she came up and also gave thanks to God. Then she told all those who were looking for the redemption of Jerusalem that she had seen Jesus, the Messiah.

Lu. 2:36-38

Women Who Came to Jesus...

...and found

Acceptance

Forgiveness

Healing

THE SYROPHENICIAN WOMAN—Who found acceptance for herself and healing for her child.

MARY—Who poured out her love.

MARY AND MARTHA—Who were each accepted in spite of their personality differences.

THE BENT WOMAN—Who was healed of a disabling handicap.

THE WOMAN AT THE WELL—Who, though of a hated ethnic origin, was accepted and forgiven.

A CHRONICALLY ILL WOMAN—Who reached out in faith, touched Jesus, and was healed.

MARY MAGDALENE—Out of whom seven demons were cast—she was honored to be one of the first to see the risen Jesus.

THE SYROPHENICIAN WOMAN—
Who found acceptance for herself and healing for her child.

A woman whose little daughter had a demon came and fell at Jesus' feet.

The woman was a Gentile, a Syrophenician. She begged him to cast the demon out of her daughter.

He said to her, "First, let the Jewish children be satisfied, for it is not good to take the children's bread and throw it to the dogs."

But she answered back saying to him, "That's true, Lord, but even the dogs under the table feed on the children's scraps."

And He said to her, "Because of your answer go on your way; the demon has gone out of your daughter."

She went back to her home, and there found the child lying on the bed. The demon had gone!

Mk. 7:25-30

MARY— *Who poured out her love.*

When Jesus was in the village of Bethany,
dining at the home of Simon the leper, a
woman came in with an alabaster flask of
very expensive perfume. She broke open
the flask and poured it over his head.

Some of the guests were indignant and re-
marked to one another, "Why has she
wasted this perfume? It could have been
sold for over three hundred denarii, and
the money given to the poor!" They
snarled at her.

But Jesus said, "Leave her alone. Why do
you embarrass her? She has done a beautiful thing to me.

"You will always have the poor with you,
and whenever you wish you can help
them; but you will not always have me here
with you.

"She has done what she could and has
anointed my body before my death and
burial.

"And I tell you this solemn truth: wherever
the Good News is preached throughout
the whole world, this woman's deed shall
be remembered."

Mk. 14:3-9

MARTHA AND MARY— *Who were each accepted in spite of their personality differences.*

Jesus entered the village of Bethany. There a woman named Martha welcomed him into her home.

Martha's sister Mary sat on the floor at Jesus' feet listening to his teaching.

But Martha was upset with all her preparations for dinner. Finally she came to Jesus and said, "Lord, don't you care that my sister has left me to do all the serving alone? Tell her to help me."

But Jesus answered her, "Martha, Martha, you are worried and bothered about so many things; but only a few things are important, really only one, and Mary has discovered it. That which she has chosen cannot be taken away from her."

Lu. 10:38-42

THE BENT WOMAN — *Who was healed of a disabling handicap.*

One Sabbath when Jesus was teaching in one of the synagogues, there was a woman who had been ill for eighteen years. She was bent double and could not straighten up at all.

When Jesus saw her, he called her over and said to her, "Woman, you are set free from your sickness!"

Then he laid his hands upon her and immediately she stood straight. She began praising and glorifying God!

Lu. 13:10-13

THE WOMAN AT THE WELL—*Who, though of a hated ethnic origin, was accepted and forgiven.*

Jesus was sitting beside a well in Samaria when a woman came there to draw water. Jesus said to her, "Give me a drink."

He was alone because his disciples had gone into the city to buy food.

She was surprised at his request. "How is it that you, a Jew, ask me for a drink since I am a Samaritan woman?" She said this because Jews have no dealings with Samaritans.

Jesus answered, "If you knew about the wonderful gift God has for you, and who it is who asks for a drink, you would have asked him and he would have given you living water."

She said to him, "But Sir, you have no rope and bucket and the well is deep. Where would you get that living water? Are you greater than our father Jacob, who gave us the well and drank of it himself along with his sons and his cattle?"

Jesus answered her, "Everyone who drinks this water will be thirsty again, but those who drink the water that I will give them will have no more thirst! The water that I give them will become a perpetual spring giving them eternal life!"

The woman said to him, "Sir, give me this water, so I will never be thirsty again and so that I will not have to come all the way out here to draw water."

"Go, get your husband and bring him here," Jesus said.

The woman said, "I have no husband."

Jesus said to her, "You have answered correctly, for you have had five husbands, and the man you are living with now is not your husband."

Startled, the woman said to him, "Sir, you must be a prophet! Our fathers worshiped here on Mount Gerazim; and you Jews say that Jerusalem is the proper place to worship."

Jesus said, "Woman, believe me, the time is coming when we will worship the Father neither in this mountain, nor in Jerusalem. You don't even understand what it is that you worship, for salvation comes from the Jews. But an hour is coming, and is here even now, when true worshipers will worship the Father in spirit and in truth. God is looking for such people.

"God is a spirit," Jesus continued, "and those who worship him must worship in spirit and truth."

The woman said to him, "I know that the Christ is coming and that when he comes, he will explain everything to us."

Jesus said to her, "I am he."

Just then his disciples returned and they were amazed that he had been speaking with a woman, and a Samaritan at that. Yet none of them asked him why.

Then the woman left her waterpot beside the well, and went back to the village where she said to the men, "Come, see a man who told me everything I ever did. Could this be the Christ?"

The men of the city came to see.

Jn. 4:7-30

A CHRONICALLY ILL WOMAN—
Who reached out in faith, touched Jesus, and was healed.

As Jesus returned, the crowd welcomed him, for they had all been waiting for him.

In the crowd was a woman who had been hemorrhaging for twelve years. She had spent her entire living on doctors and could not be healed by anyone. Instead of getting better, she got worse.

She had heard about the wonderful miracles Jesus was doing and said to herself, "If only I can touch his robe, I will be healed." So she came up behind him, and touched just the fringe of his cloak. Immediately her hemorrhaging stopped!

Jesus was conscious that power had gone out from him. "Who touched my clothes?" he asked.

His disciples answered, "Do you see the crowd pressing you on all sides and you say, 'Who touched me?' "

But Jesus looked around to see who had done it. Then the woman, afraid and trembling, knowing full well what had happened to her, stepped forward, fell at his feet, and told him the whole truth.

"Daughter," he said to her, "your faith has made you well. Go in peace."

Mk. 5:25-34

MARY MAGDALENE—*Out of whom seven demons were cast—she was one of the first to see the risen Jesus.*

When evening came, Joseph of Arimathea took the body of Jesus, wrapped it in a clean linen cloth, and laid it in his own new rock-hewn tomb. Then he rolled a large stone across the entrance and went away.

There were many women there who had been taking care of Jesus and had followed him from Galilee to Jerusalem. Among them was Mary Magdalene, along with Mary the mother of James and Joseph, and also the mother of James and John, the sons of Zebedee.

After the Sabbath day ended, just as Sunday was dawning, Mary Magdalene went to the grave.

Suddenly there was a severe earthquake. For an angel of the Lord had come down from heaven and rolled away the stone.

So Mary ran to tell Peter and John. She said to them, "They have taken away the Lord out of the tomb, and we do not know where they have laid him."

Upon hearing this, Peter and John ran to the tomb. When they arrived they stooped and looked in and saw the linen grave clothes lying there. They did not understand the scripture that said Jesus must rise again from the dead. They went on home.

By this time Mary had returned and now stood outside the tomb and wept. As she was crying she stooped down and looked into the tomb and saw two angels in white.

One was sitting at the head and one at the foot of the place where the body of Jesus had been lying.

"Woman, why are you crying?" they said to her.

"Because they have taken away my Lord's body and I do not know where they have laid him."

As she said this, she turned around and saw someone standing behind her. She did not realize it was Jesus.

He said to her, "Woman, why are you weeping? Whom are you seeking?"

Mary, still thinking he was the gardener, said to him, "Sir, if you have taken him away, tell me where you have laid him, I will go get him and take him away."

Jesus said to her, "Mary!"

She turned quickly and said, "Master!"

Jesus said, "Stop clinging to me, for I have not yet ascended to the Father. Go to the disciples and say to them, I ascend to my Father and your Father, to my God and your God."

Mary Magdalene found the disciples and told them, "I have seen the Lord!" Then she told them all that the Lord had said to her.

Mt. 27:54-57, 59-61; Jn. 20:1-18

GOD'S HONOR ROLL OF WOMEN

Women of

Faith

Courage

Strength

Commitment

Kindness

Charity

Hospitality

Wisdom

SARAH—Who believed God for a son despite her age and the impossibility of her situation.

SHIPHRAH AND PUAH—Two brave women who revered God and courageously defied Pharoah's orders.

JOCHEBED—Who trusted God with her child's life.

RAHAB THE HARLOT—Who received God's forgiveness and was taken into the lineage of Jesus.

RUTH—A faithful, foreign-born daughter-in-law, who became an ancestress of Jesus.

HANNAH—Who believed God for a child.

ESTHER—Who courageously trusted God and saved her people from destruction.

DORCAS—A woman of Christian kindness and charity.

LYDIA—Who practiced Christian hospitality.

PRISCILLA—Who taught others about God's word.

EUNICE AND LOIS—Who taught a young man their faith.

SARAH— *Who, though childless, believed God for a son despite her age and the impossibility of her situation.*

Then God said to Abraham, "As for Sarai your wife, you shall not call her Sarai anymore. Her name will be Sarah [Princess].

"And I will bless her, and I will give you a son by her. I will bless her so that she shall be a mother of nations. Kings of people shall come from her."

Then Abraham fell on his face and laughed, and said in his heart, "Will a child be born to a man one hundred years old? And will Sarah, who is ninety years old, bear a child?"

God said, "Sarah your wife is about to bear you a son, and you shall name him Isaac [He laughs]. I am going to establish my covenant with him forever and with his descendants after him."

Gen 17:15-17, 19

Then the Lord did as he promised and Sarah conceived and bore a son to Abraham in his old age, at the appointed time God had mentioned to him.

Gen 21:1, 2

By faith even Sarah herself received ability to conceive, even though it was beyond the child-bearing time of her life, because she regarded him who had promised to be faithful. And so from one man, and he was already impotent, came as many descendants as the stars of heaven and they were as innumerable as the sand on the seashore.

Heb. 11:11, 12

SHIPHRAH AND PUAH—*Two women who revered God and courageously defied Pharoah's orders.*

The king of Egypt spoke to the Hebrew midwives, one of whom was named Shiphrah and the other was named Puah. He said to them, "When you are helping the Hebrew women give birth, watch them closely upon the birthstool. If it is a son, put him to death; but if it is a daughter, let her live."

But the midwives revered God, and did not do as the king of Egypt commanded them. They let the boys live, too.

So the king of Egypt called for them again, and said to them, "Why have you let the male babies live?"

The midwives said to Pharoah, "Because the Hebrew women are not like the Egyptian women. They are very vigorous, and they give birth before the midwife can get to them."

God was good to the midwives, and the people multiplied, and became very mighty. And because the midwives feared God, he gave them children of their own.

Ex. 1:15-21

JOCHEBED — *Who trusted God with her child's life.*

Then Pharoah commanded all his people, saying, "Every boy baby born is to be cast into the Nile River, and every girl baby you are to keep alive."

A man from the Levite tribe married a Levite maiden by the name of Jochebed.

In time the woman conceived and bore a son. When she saw him, she saw that he was beautiful, and so instead of killing him, she hid him for three months. But finally, she could hide him no longer, and so she got a wicker basket and covered it over with tar and pitch. Then she put the child into it, and set it among the reeds by the bank of the Nile. The baby's sister stood nearby to find out what would happen to him.

Then the Pharoah's daughter came down to bathe. While she was bathing her maidens walked alongside the river. Suddenly she saw the basket among the reeds and sent her maid to bring it to her.

When she opened it, she saw the baby boy and he was crying. She had pity on him and said, "This is one of the Hebrews' children."

Then the baby's sister said to Pharaoh's daughter, "Shall I go and call a nurse for you from the Hebrew women, that she may nurse the child for you?"

Pharaoh's daughter said to her, "Go ahead." So the girl went and called the baby's own mother, Jochebed.

Then Pharaoh's daughter said to Jochebed, "Take this child away and nurse him for me and I shall pay you wages." So the woman took the child and nursed him.

The child grew, and eventually Jochebed brought him to Pharoah's daughter, and he became her son. She named him Moses [drawn out], "Because," she said, "I drew him out of the water."

Ex. l:22; 2:1-20

RAHAB THE HARLOT— *Who received God's forgiveness and was taken into the lineage of Jesus.*

Then Joshua the son of Nun sent two men from Acacia to spy out the land. He said, "Go, survey the land, especially Jericho." So they went to Jericho where they came into the house of a harlot named Rahab. They stayed there.

But it was reported to the king of Jericho, "Men from Israel have come here tonight to spy out the land."

Then the king of Jericho sent word to Rahab, "Bring out the men who have come to your house, for they have come to spy out the entire land."

But Rahab had hidden the two men. She said, "Yes, the men came to me, but I did not know where they came from.

"At dark, when it was time to shut the gate, the men went out. I don't know where they went. Pursue them quickly, for you can still overtake them!"

However, the truth was that she had brought them up to the roof and hidden them under the stalks of flax which she had laid out there.

So the king's men pursued them on the road to the Jordan River as far as the fords. Just as soon as those who were pursuing the two spies had gone out, the gatekeeper shut the gate.

Now before the two men retired for the night, Rahab came up to them on the roof and said to them, "I know that the Lord has given you the land, and that terror has fallen on all of us. I know that all the inhabitants of the land have melted away in fear before you.

"For we have heard how the Lord dried up the water of the Red Sea before you when you came out of Egypt, and what you did to the two Amorite kings on the other side of the Jordan, and also to Sihon and Og, whom you completely destroyed.

"When we heard it, our hearts melted from fear. There was no courage left in any man because of you. For the Lord your God, he is God in heavens above and on earth beneath.

"So now, please swear to me by the Lord, that because I have been kind to you, that you also will be kind to my father's household. Give me a pledge of good faith that you will spare my father, my mother, my brothers, and my sisters, and all who belong to them. Save us from death!"

So the men said to her, "If you do not tell this business of ours we will deal kindly with you when the Lord gives us the land. Our promise is our life for yours!"

Then she let them down through the window by a rope, for her house was on the city wall.

She said to them, "Go to the hill country or your pursuers may find you. Hide there for three days until the pursuers return here. Then you may go on your way."

The men said to her, "We may be released from this oath we made to you, unless when we come into the land, you tie this scarlet cord in the same window through which you let us down. Gather your father, your mother, your brothers and sisters, and all their households into your house."

"If anyone goes out of your house into the street, his blood will be on his own head. But we shall be innocent. But with regard to anyone who is in the house with you, his blood shall be on our head, if a hand is laid on him.

"And if you expose this secret mission of ours, then we will be released from the oath which you made us swear."

And she said, "Let it be according to your terms." So she sent them away. When they had departed, she tied the scarlet cord in the window.

On the seventh day of the siege, the Hebrews rose and at dawn marched around the city of Jericho in the same manner as they had done six times before; only on that day they marched around the city not once, but seven times.

On the seventh time, the priests blew the trumpets and Joshua said to the people, "Shout! For the Lord has given you the city.

"And the city and all that is in it belongs to the Lord. Only Rahab the harlot, and all who are with her in her house shall live, because she hid the spies whom we sent."

Joshua said to the two men who had spied out the land, "Go now into the harlot's house and bring her and all she has out of there, just as you promised to do."

So the young men who were spies went in and brought out Rahab and her father and mother, and her brothers and the rest of her relatives, and placed them outside the camp of Israel.

Then the Hebrews burned Jericho and everything in it. Only the silver and gold and articles of bronze and iron were saved. These they put into the treasury of the house of the Lord.

Rahab the harlot and her father's household and all she had were spared and she has lived in the midst of Israel to this day for she hid the messengers whom Joshua sent to spy out Jericho.

Josh. 2:1-21, 6:15-17, 22, 25

Here is the geneology of Jesus Christ, the son of David...and to Salmon was born Boaz by *Rahab*; and to Boaz was born Obed by Ruth; and to Obed, Jesse; and to Jesse was born David the king.

Mt. 1:1, 5

By faith Rahab the harlot did not die along with those who were disobedient, because she had welcomed the spies in peace.

Heb. 11:31

You see that a man is justified by works, and not by faith alone. And in the same way was not Rahab the harlot also justified by works, when she received the messengers and sent them out by another way?

Jas. 2:25

RUTH—*A faithful, foreign-born daughter-in-law, who became an ancestress of Jesus.*

Then Naomi decided to return from the Land of Moab where she had been living. Her daughters-in-law went with her. She had heard while living in the land of Moab that the Lord had provided his chosen people with food.

So she left the place where she was, and started out on the way which would lead to the land of Judah.

After a while, Naomi said to her two daughters- in-law, "Go back each of you to your mother's house. May the Lord deal as kindly with you as you have dealt with your dead husbands, my sons, and with me.

"May the Lord help each of you find rest, each in the house of her husband." Then she kissed them goodbye, but they lifted up their voices and wept.

Ruth, one of the two daughters-in-law said, "Do not urge me to leave you or turn back from following you; for where you go, I will go, and where you lodge, I will lodge. Your people shall be my people, and your God, my God.

"Where you die, I will die, and there I will be buried. May the Lord do so to me, and worse, if anything but death parts you and me."

After a time Boaz, a near relative, took Ruth as his wife. In due time the Lord enabled her to conceive, and she gave birth to a son.

Then the woman said to Naomi, "Blessed is the Lord who has given you this grandson. May he become famous in Israel.

"May he rejuvenate you and sustain you in your old age; for your daughter-in-law, Ruth, who loves you and is better to you than seven sons, has given birth to him."

Ruth 1:11-6-8, 14-17, 4:13-15

Here is the geneology of Jesus Christ, the Son of David ... and to Salmon was born Boaz by Rahab; and to Boaz was born Obed by *Ruth*; and to Obed, Jesse; and to Jesse was born David the king.

Mt. 1:1, 5

HANNAH — *Who believed God for a child.*

There was a man from the hill country of Ephraim by the name of Elkanah. He had two wives: Hannah and Peninnah. Peninnah had children, but Hannah had none.

Every year this man would go up from his city to Shiloh to worship and to sacrifice to the Lord.

On the day that Elkanah sacrificed, he would give presents to Peninnah and to all her sons and daughters. To Hannah he would give a double present for he loved Hannah even though the Lord had closed her womb.

Her rival, however, would provoke her mercilessly just to irritate her, because the Lord had closed her womb. This happened year after year, every time as often as she went to the house of the Lord, she would provoke her, until she wept and could not eat.

Then Elkanah her husband said, "Hannah, why do you weep and why do you not eat? Why are you so sad? Am I not better to you than ten sons?"

One evening Hannah rose after dinner when they were in Shiloh. She went to the tabernacle. At the time Eli the priest was sitting by the doorpost of the Lord's temple.

Hannah was greatly distressed and she prayed to the Lord, weeping bitterly. She made a vow saying "O Lord of hosts, if you will look on my trouble and remember me, and will give me a son, then I will give him to you for the rest of his life. No razor shall ever be used on his head."

As she continued praying before the Lord, Eli was watching her mouth. Hannah was speaking in her heart. Only her lips were moving, but her voice was not heard. So Eli thought she was drunk!

He said to her, "Must you come here drunk? Get rid of your wine."

But Hannah said, "No, my lord, I am a deeply grieved woman. I have drunk no wine nor any other liquor, but I have poured out my soul before the Lord.

"Do not consider me worthless, for I have spoken out of my great concern and provocation."

The Eli said, "Go in peace; and may the God of Israel grant what you have asked of Him."

Then she said, "Let your maidservant find favor in your sight." So Hannah went on her way; she ate, and her face showed no more sadness.

In the morning they rose early, worshiped before the Lord, and then returned to their house in Ramah. When Elkanah had relations with Hannah his wife, the Lord remembered her. And in due time, Hannah conceived and gave birth to a son. She named him Samuel, "Because I have asked him of the Lord."

The next year when Elkanah went up with all his household to offer to the Lord the yearly sacrifice and pay his vow, Hannah did not go. She said to him "I will not go up again until the child is weaned; then I will take him, so that he may appear before the Lord and stay there forever.

And Elkanah her husband said to her, "All right, do what seems best to you. Stay home until you have weaned him and may the Lord confirm his word." So Hannah stayed at home and nursed her son until she weaned him.

When she had weaned him, she took him, still very young, with her to the Lord's house in Shiloh. She also took a three-year-old bull, one bushel of flour, and a skin of wine.

There they slaughtered the bull for a sacrifice. Hannah then brought the boy to Eli. She said, "Oh, my lord!" I am the woman who stood here beside you, praying to the Lord for this boy. He has granted my request. So I have dedicated this child to him for as long as he lives."

Then Elkanah and Hannah went home to Ramah. But the boy was in the Lord's service under the direction of Eli the priest.

1 Sam.1:1-28; 2:11

THE SHUNAMMITE WOMAN — *Who had faith even when her young son died.*

One day when Elisha went to Shunem, where there was a prominent woman. She persuaded him to stay for lunch. After that as often as he passed by, he stopped there for a meal.

She said to her husband, "Truly, I know that this man is a holy man of God.

"Please, let us make a little walled upstairs chamber and let us put in a bed, a table, a chair, and a lampstand. Whenever he comes to us he can rest there."

One day when he came to Shunem, he stopped to rest in the upper bedroom. He said to Gehazi his servant, "Call the woman." And she came and stood before him.

Then Elisha said to Gehazi, "Tell her, we appreciate her care and kindness. What can I do for her? Can I make a request of the king or the captain of the army?"

She answered, "I am content. I live among my own people."

So he said, "What then can we do for her?" Gehazi answered, "She has no son and her husband is old."

He said, "Call her back again." When she came, she stood in the doorway. Then Elisha said, "At this same time next year, you shall embrace a son." And she said, "No, my lord, Do not lie to me."

But the woman conceived and bore a son at that same season the next year, just as Elisha had said she would.

One day when the child was older, he went out with his father and the reapers. He cried out to his father, "My head! My head!" His father said to his servant, "Take him to his mother."

So he took the boy to his mother. He sat on her lap until noon and then died. She went up and laid him on Elisha's bed and shut the door behind her, and went out.

Then she called her husband and said, "Please send me one of the servants and one of the donkeys. I'm going to Elisha."

And he said, "Why are you going to him today? This isn't a religious holiday."

She said, "It will be well."

Then she saddled a donkey and said to her servant, "Go quickly and don't slow down the pace for me unless I tell you." She hurried along until she came to Elisha who was at Mount Carmel.

Elisha looked up and saw her at a distance. He said to Gehazi his servant, "Look there is the Shunammite. Please run to meet her and say to her, 'Is it well with you? Is it well with your husband? Is it well with the child?'" When Gehazi did this the woman answered, "It is well."

But when she came to Elisha at the hill, she embraced his feet. Gehazi came near to push her away; but Elisha said, "Let her alone, for her soul is deeply troubled, and the Lord has not told me what is wrong."

Then she said, "Did I ask you for a son? Didn't I say, 'Don't give me false hope?'"

Then he said to Gehazi, "Quick! Take my staff in your hand and go! If you meet anyone, don't talk. When you arrive, lay my staff on the lad's face."

And the woman said, "As the Lord lives, I will not go home without you." So he got up and went with her.

Gehazi had preceded them and had laid the staff on the lad's face, as instructed. But there was no sound nor response. So he started back and met Elisha and the woman and said, "The lad has not awakened."

When Elisha came into the house, he found the lad was dead and laid on his bed. So he entered the room and shut the door behind him. Then he prayed to the Lord.

He stretched out upon the child, putting his mouth on the child's mouth and his eyes on the child's eyes, and his hands on the child's hands; and the child became warm.

Then he came down and walked back and forth in the house. Then he went up again and stretched himself on the lad again. At that the boy sneezed seven times and opened his eyes.

Elisha called Gehazi and told him, "Call the Shunammite." So he called her. And when she came up to Elisha, he said, "Here is your son!"

She fell at his feet, bowing herself to the ground in thanksgiving. Then she picked up her son and went out.

2 Kin. 4:8-37

ESTHER THE QUEEN — *Who courageously trusted God and saved her people from destruction.*

There was a Jew in Susa the capital of Persia, whose name was Mordecai. He had been taken into exile along with the other captives from Jerusalem in the time of Jeconiah the king.

He was raising Esther, his cousin, as if she were his own daughter, for she was an orphan. Now Esther was extremely beautiful of form and face.

One day the king issued a command to gather for consideration all the eligible young maidens in the land. One of them would become the queen of Persia. Esther was one who was taken to the king's palace and put into the custody of Hegai who was in charge of the women.

Esther pleased him so much that he quickly provided her with cosmetics, food, and gave her seven choice maids from the king's palace. Then he transferred her and her maids to the best place in the harem.

But Esther told no one that she was a Jew, because Mordecai had told her she must not.

After twelve months of preparation, when her turn came, Esther went before the king in his royal palace.

And the king loved Esther more than all the women brought before him. She found favor and kindness with him. He set the royal crown upon her head and made her queen.

It was about that time that two of the king's officials from among those who guarded the door, became angry and sought to kill the king. But the plot became known to Mordecai and he told Queen Esther. She then, informed the king what was happening.

When the plot was investigated and found to be true, both the officials were hanged on gallows in the king's presence.

Soon afterwards, the king promoted a man named Haman over all the princes of the land. Everyone was told to bow down and pay homage to him. But Mordecai refused to do so.

This filled Haman with rage. And he convinced the king to issue a decree to have the people of Mordecai, the Jews, all put to death because they would not obey the law and bow down to Haman. "I will even pay

$20,000,000 into the treasury for the expenses involved in this purge," Haman said.

When Mordecai learned all that had happened, he wept loudly and bitterly in the streets. Esther heard about it and sent to ask Mordecai why he wept so.

Mordecai sent back a message telling all that had happened to him. He told her the exact amount of money that Haman had promised to pay the king's treasuries for the destruction of the Jews, and he also sent her a copy of the edict which had been issued for their destruction.

Esther then sent a message back to Mordecai saying, "I can't do anything. The king has but one law, that anyone coming to him who is not summoned will be put to death unless when he comes, the king holds out to him a golden scepter. And I have not been summoned to the king for thirty days".

Then Mordecai replied to Esther. "Don't think that you in the king's palace can escape any more than all the rest of the Jews. For if you remain silent at this time, deliverance for the Jews will come from another place and you and your father's house will be destroyed. And who knows whether you have not attained royalty for such a time as this?"

Then Esther sent word to Moredcai, "Go, gather all the Jews who are in Susa and fast for me. We will fast here, too. Then I will go in to the king, which is not according to the law; and if I die, I die!"

So Esther took courage and putting on her finest royal robes, went into the inner court of the king's palace.

When the king saw Esther standing there, he was pleased. He extended to her the golden scepter. She came near and touched the top of the scepter.

"What's wrong, Esther?" the king asked. "Whatever your request is, I will give it to you, even to half of the kingdom."

So Esther invited the king to bring Haman and come to a series of banquets. At the last banquet the king once again asked Esther what it was that she wanted.

Then she said, "If I have pleased you, O king, let me live and my people as well, for we have been sold to be destroyed."

"Who is he, and where is he that would presume to do this?" the king asked.

Esther then named Haman. And Haman became terrified before the king and queen.

The king in his anger rushed out of the palace to the garden. While he was gone, Haman fell upon Esther's couch pleading for his life. At that moment the king returned and saw him there. "Will he rape the queen before my own eyes in my own house?"

As the word left the king's mouth, they placed a death veil over Haman's face. One of the servants told the king about the gallows upon which Haman had intended to hang Mordecai.

The king said, "Hang him on it!" And that is what they did.

Then Mordecai put on the royal robes of blue and white, with a large crown of gold and a garment of fine linen and purple and went out. The whole city of Susa shouted and rejoiced!

And the Jews had light and gladness, joy and honor!

Similarly in each and every province, and in every city, wherever the king's mandate and decree arrived, there was gladness and joy for the Jews. It was a feast and a holiday! Many among the people of the land became Jews, because fear of the Jews had come upon them.

(Paraphrased from the book of Esther.)

DORCAS—*A woman of Christian kindness and charity.*

In the town of Joppa there was a woman named Dorcas; this woman was continually doing deeds of kindness and charity.

One day she became ill and died. Her friends washed her body and laid it in an upstairs room.

And since Lydda was near Joppa, the disciples, having heard that Peter was there, sent two men to beg him, "Do not delay! Come quickly to us!"

Peter got up and came to Joppa. And when they arrived, they took him to the upstairs room. There all the widows stood around weeping, showing him all the coats and garments that Dorcas had made while she was living.

Peter sent them all out and knelt down and prayed. Then turning to the body, he said, "Dorcas, arise!" She opened her eyes, and when she saw Peter, she sat up.

Giving her his hand he helped her up and called in all the saints and widows. He presented her alive to them. This became known all over Joppa, and many believed in the Lord.

Ac.: 9:36-42

LYDIA— *Who practiced Christian hospitality.*

Paul was preaching in Phillipi and a woman named Lydia, from the city of Thyatira, a seller of purple fabrics and a worshiper of God, sat listening. The Lord opened her heart to respond to the things spoken by Paul.

When she and her family had been baptized, she urged Paul, saying, "If you have judged me to be faithful to the Lord, come into my house and stay." She prevailed upon us to come.

Sometime later, after Paul and Silas had been in prison, they went again to the house of Lydia, and when they saw the brethren, they encouraged them and then departed.

Ac. 16:14, 15, 40

PRISCILLA— *Who taught others about God's word.*

Paul left Athens and went to the city of Corinth.

There he found a certain Jew named Aquila, a native of Pontus, who had recently come from Italy with his wife, Priscilla, because Claudius had commanded all the Jews to leave Rome.

Paul called on them because they were of the same trade, tent-makers. He stayed with them and they worked together.

Later on, a certain Jew named Apollos, an Alexandrian by birth, an eloquent man and powerful in the scriptures, came to Ephesus.

This man had been instructed in the way of the Lord. He was fervent in spirit, and he was speaking and teaching accurately all the things concerning Jesus. However he was acquainted only with the baptism of John. He began to speak out boldly in the synagogue. But when Priscilla and Aquila heard him, they took him aside and explained the way of God more accurately to him.

Ac. 18: 2, 3, 18, 24, 25

The churches of Asia greet you, Aquila and Priscilla greet you heartily in the Lord, along with the church that meets in their house.

1 Cor. 16:19

EUNICE AND LOIS—*Who passed on their faith.*

Timothy: I, Paul, remind you of the sincere faith you have, which lived first in your grandmother Lois, and in your mother Eunice, and I am sure is living in you as well.

2 Tim. 1:5

GOD'S PROMISES TO WOMEN

To the Fearful

Of Wisdom

When You Feel
  Abandoned

To Help Women

When Your Children
  Leave Home

Of Security

To Poor Women

When Praying for Your
  Children

Let your conversation be without covetousness; and be content with such things as you have: for he has said, I will never leave you, nor forsake you.

Heb. 13:5

Christ is able for all time to save those who draw near to God through him, since he always lives to make intercession for them.

Heb. 7:25 RSV

I know whom I have believed, and am persuaded that he is able to keep that which I've committed unto him against that day.

2 Tim. 1:12

I am with you and will watch over you wherever you go, and I will bring you back to this land. I will not leave you until I have done what I have promised you.

Gen 28:15 NIV

And he said, My presence shall go with you, and I will give you rest.

Ex. 33:14

Be strong and courageous. Do not be afraid or terrified because of them, for the Lord your God goes with you; he will never leave you nor forsake you.

Deut. 31:6 NIV

I am with you says the Lord.

Hag. 1:13

No one will be able to stand up against you all the days of your life. As I was with Moses, so I will be with you; I will never leave you or forsake you.

Josh. 1:5 NIV

Teaching them to observe all things I commanded you: and, lo, I am with you always, even unto the end of the world.

Mt. 28:20

Be perfect, be of good comfort, be of one mind, live in peace, and the God of love and peace shall be with you.

2 Cor. 13:11

Those things, which you have both learned, and received, and heard, and seen in me, do: and the God of peace shall be with you.

Phil. 4:9

What person is he that fears the Lord? Him shall he teach in the way that he shall choose.

Ps. 25:12

The steps of a good person are ordered by the Lord: and he delights in his way. Though he fall, he shall not be utterly cast down: for the Lord upholds him with his hand.

Ps. 37:23-24

For this God is our God for ever and ever: He will be our guide even unto death.

Ps. 48:14

Trust in the Lord with all your heart; and lean not unto your own understanding. In all your ways acknowledge him, and he shall direct your paths.

Pr. 3:5-6

For the Lord gives wisdom: out of his mouth comes knowledge and understanding.

Pr. 2:6

When wisdom enters into your heart, and knowledge is pleasant unto your soul; discretion shall preserve you, understanding shall keep you.

Pr. 2:10-11

If any of you lacks wisdom, let him ask of God, that gives to all men generously and without reproach, and it will be given to him.

Jas. 1:5 NASB

I know whom I have believed, and am persuaded that he is able to keep that which I've committed unto him against that day.

2 Tim. 1:12

No one will be able to stand up against you all the days of your life. As I was with Moses, so I will be with you; I will never leave you or forsake you.

Josh. 1:5 NIV

Let your conversation be without covetousness; and be content with such things as you have: for he has said, I will never leave you, nor forsake you.

Heb. 13:5

Know therefore that the Lord your God, he is God, the faithful God, who keeps covenant and mercy with them that love him and keep his commandments.

Deut. 7:9

He is faithful that promised.

Heb. 10:23

But if from then you shall seek the Lord your God, you shall find him, if you seek him with all your heart and all your soul.

Deut. 4:29

For the Lord searches all hearts, and understands all the imaginations of the thoughts: if you seek him, he will be found of you.

1 Chr. 28:9

The Lord is with you, while you are with him; and if you seek him, he will be found of you.

2 Chr. 15:2

The hand of our God is upon all them for good that seek him.

Ezr. 8:32

They that seek the Lord shall not lack any good thing.

Ps. 34:10

The Lord is nigh unto all them that call upon him, to all that call upon him in truth.

Ps. 145:18

And you shall seek me, and find me, when you shall search for me with all your heart.

Jer. 29:13

Blessed are they which do hunger and search after righteousness: for they shall be filled.

Mt. 5:6

But seek first the kingdom of God, and his righteousness; and all these things shall be added unto you.

Mt. 6:33

Now faith is the substance of things hoped for, the evidence of things not seen. ...Through faith we understand that the world was framed by the word of God...but without faith it is impossible to please him: for he that comes to God must believe that he is, and that he is a rewarder of them that diligently seek him.

Heb. 11:1, 3, 6

I know whom I have believed, and am persuaded that he is able to keep that which I've committed unto him against that day.

2 Tim 1:12

Now to him who is able to keep you from falling and to present you without blemish before the presence of his glory with rejoicing, to the only God our Savior through Jesus Christ our Lord, be glory, majesty, dominion, and authority, before all time, and now, and forever. Amen.

Jude 24, 25

Let your conversation be without covetousness; and be content with such things as you have: For he has said, I will never leave you, nor forsake you.

Heb. 13:5

But he that shall endure unto the end, the same shall be saved.

Mt. 24:13

God will render to every man according to his deeds: to them who by patient continuance in well doing seek for glory and honour and immortality, God will render eternal life.

Rom. 2:6, 7

Therefore, my beloved brethren, be steadfast, unmovable, always abounding in the work of the Lord, forasmuch as you know that your labour is not in vain in the Lord.

1 Cor. 15:58

It shall come to pass, when he cries unto me, that I will hear; for I am gracious.

Ex. 22:27

He delivers the poor in his affliction, and opens their ears in oppression.

Job 36:15

For the oppression of the poor, for the sighing of the needy, now will I arise, says the Lord; I will set him in safety from him that threatens him.

Ps. 12:5

All my bones shall say, Lord, who is like unto you, which delivers the poor from him that is too strong for him, yes, the poor and the needy from him that spoils him?

Ps. 35:10

For the Lord hears the poor, and despises not his prisoners.

Ps. 69:33

He shall judge the people with righteousness, and the poor with judgement. He shall judge the poor of the people, he shall save the children of the needy, and shall break in pieces the oppressor.

Ps. 72:2, 4

For he shall deliver the needy when he cries; the poor also, and him that has no helper. He shall spare the poor and needy, and shall save the souls of the needy.

Ps. 72:12-13

For he shall stand at the right hand of the poor, to save him from those that condemn his soul.

Ps. 109:31

I will abundantly bless her provision: I will satisfy her poor with bread.

Ps. 132:15

Rob not the poor, because he is poor: neither oppress the afflicted in the gate: for the Lord will plead their cause, and spoil the soul of those that spoiled them.

Pr. 22:22-23

When the poor and needy seek water, and there is none, and their tongue fails for thirst, I the Lord will hear them, I the God of Israel will not forsake them.

Isa. 41:17

If my people, which are called by my name, shall humble themselves, and pray, and seek my face, and turn from their wicked ways; then will I hear from heaven, and will forgive their sin, and will heal their land.

2 Chr. 7:14

You shall make your prayer unto him, and he shall hear you.

Job 22:27

He will fulfill the desire of them that fear him: he will also hear their cry, and will save them.

Ps. 145:19

The Lord is far from the wicked: but he hears the prayer of the righteous.

Pr. 15:29

Then shall you call, and the Lord will answer; you shall cry, and he shall say, "Here I am."

Isa. 58:9

Before they call, I will answer; and while they are yet speaking, I will hear.

Isa. 65:24

Then shall you call upon me, and you shall go and pray unto me, and I will hearken unto you.

Jer. 29:12

Call unto me, and I will answer you, and show you great and mighty things, which you know not.

Jer. 33:3

When you pray, enter into your closet, and when you have shut the door, pray to the Father which is in secret; and your Father which sees in secret shall reward you openly.

Mt. 6:6

Ask, and it shall be given you; seek, and you shall find; knock, and it shall be opened unto you. For every one that asks, receives; and he that seeks, finds; and to him that knocks, it shall be opened....How much more shall your Father which is in heaven give good things to them that ask him?

Mt. 7:7-8, 11

All things whatsoever you shall ask in prayer, believing, you shall receive.

Mt. 11:24

If two of you shall agree on earth as touching anything that they shall ask, it shall be done for them of my Father which is in heaven. For where two or three are gathered together in my name, there am I in the midst.

Mt. 18:19-20

With God all things are possible.

Mt. 19:26

And all things, whatsoever you shall ask in prayer, believing, you shall receive.

Mt. 21:22

Truly I say to you, whoever says to this mountain, be taken up and cast into the sea, and does not doubt in his heart, but believes that what he says will come to pass, it will be done for him. Therefore I tell you, whatever you ask in prayer, believe that you have received it, and it will be yours.

Mk. 11:23-24 RSV

And whatsoever you shall ask in my name, that will I do, that the Father may be glorified in the Son: if you ask anything in my name, I will do it.

Jn. 14:13-14

If you abide in me, and my words abide in you, ask what you will, and it shall be done unto you.

Jn. 15:7

You have not chosen me, but I have chosen you, and ordained you, that you should go and bring forth fruit, and that your fruit should remain: that whatsoever you shall ask of the Father in my name, he may give it to you.

Jn. 15:16

My Father will give you whatever you ask in my name. Until now you have not asked for anything in my name. Ask and you will receive, and your joy will be complete.

Jn. 16:23-24 NIV

If any of you lack wisdom, let him ask of God, who gives to all men generously and without reproach, and it will be given to him.

Jas. 1:5

And whatsoever we ask, we receive of him, because we keep his commandments, and do those things that are pleasing in his sight.

1 Jn. 3:22

And this is the confidence that we have in him, that, if we ask anything according to his will, he hears us.

1 Jn. 5:14